IN THE
NATIONAL INTEREST

General Sir John Monash once exhorted a graduating class to 'equip yourself for life, not solely for your own benefit but for the benefit of the whole community'. At the university established in his name, we repeat this statement to our own graduating classes, to acknowledge how important it is that common or public good flows from education.

Universities spread and build on the knowledge they acquire through scholarship in many ways, well beyond the transmission of this learning through education. It is a necessary part of a university's role to debate its findings, not only with other researchers and scholars, but also with the broader community in which it resides.

Publishing for the benefit of society is an important part of a university's commitment to free intellectual inquiry. A university provides civil space for such inquiry by its scholars, as well as for investigations by public intellectuals and expert practitioners.

This series, In the National Interest, embodies Monash University's mission to extend knowledge and encourage informed debate about matters of great significance to Australia's future.

Professor Margaret Gardner AC
President and Vice-Chancellor,
Monash University

RICHARD DENNISS

BIG: THE ROLE OF THE STATE IN THE MODERN ECONOMY

MONASH UNIVERSITY PUBLISHING

Big: The Role of the State in the Modern Economy
© Copyright 2022 Richard Denniss

Monash University Publishing
Matheson Library Annexe
40 Exhibition Walk
Monash University
Clayton, Victoria 3800, Australia
https://publishing.monash.edu

Monash University Publishing brings to the world publications which advance the best traditions of humane and enlightened thought.

ISBN: 9781922633033 (paperback)
ISBN: 9781922633057 (ebook)

Series: In the National Interest
Editor: Louise Adler
Project manager & copyeditor: Paul Smitz
Designer: Peter Long
Typesetter: Cannon Typesetting
Proofreader: Gillian Armitage
Printed in Australia by Ligare Book Printers

A catalogue record for this book is available from the National Library of Australia.

The paper this book is printed on is in accordance with the standards of the Forest Stewardship Council®. The FSC® promotes environmentally responsible, socially beneficial and economically viable management of the world's forests.

BIG: THE ROLE OF THE STATE IN THE MODERN ECONOMY

Australia's public sector isn't big enough to meet the challenges of the twenty-first century, good enough to meet the expectations of the Australian public, or well governed enough to cope with the inevitable expansion heading its way. The unfounded anxiety that Australian public spending is too high has dominated national conversations since the 1990s, even though it has no basis in fact and it no longer dominates government decision-making. The Australian public sector is growing and will continue to do so, but the determination to deny this obvious fact dampens any genuine public debate about what Australians want more of, what they want less of, and how best to pay for the services they desire.

No other country has been as insecure, or obsessed, with the existence and size of its budget surpluses. The last leaders in the United States and United Kingdom to deliver a budget surplus were Bill Clinton and Tony Blair, but no-one in those countries cares. The sky hasn't fallen, the foreign exchange markets haven't punished them, and the political right still demands big tax cuts despite the big deficits. And, contrary to twenty-five years of Australian economic orthodoxy, the richest, happiest and healthiest group of countries has the world's highest tax rates and public sectors much larger than Australia's. The Nordic countries, with their 'bloated' public sectors and 'burdensome' taxes, have also delivered faster productivity growth than Australia. While we have moved on from 'don't mention the war' and 'the inconvenient truth' of climate change, the Nordic countries remain the policy examples whose names we dare not speak.

The idea that the smaller the public sector, the more efficient the economy, is completely without foundation. Just as economics is silent on how much is too much to spend on a bottle of wine, it is also silent on how much a country should spend on its health, education and welfare systems as well. While economists might encourage you to shop around for the best price for your favourite drop, never go out for dinner with someone who thinks you should always buy the cheapest wine or have the smallest public sector possible. If nothing else, you know they aren't any good at economics.

People who don't like wine, cruising holidays or sports cars shouldn't buy them, and countries that don't want to provide high-quality health, education and transport to their citizens shouldn't provide them. But while there are plenty of countries that adopt that approach, there is absolutely no evidence that most Australians want to emulate them. Just as people can set arbitrary caps on how much they want to spend on Uber Eats each week, or on their holidays each year, the Morrison government has set a cap of 23.9 per cent on how much of our national income it wants to collect in tax and spend on services. But like the decision to spend no more than, say, $50 per week on home-delivered meals, Scott Morrison's cap on public spending is as baseless as it is precise.

Each year, Australians spend around $8 billion on coffee, about $2 billion on bottled water, and $1 billion on sports cars—even though the maximum speed limit is 110 kilometres per hour for all vehicles. While some people believe such spending is 'wasteful', economists have no such concern. As a rule, we tend to think that individuals are best placed to decide how to spend their money, and that applies when we work together as well. So if a majority of Australians vote to collect more in tax and, as a nation, spend more on public services and less on coffee and sports cars, most economists think that is just fine. But to listen to Australian public debate, you'd be forgiven for thinking economists believe that public spending destroys jobs, growth and innovation.

There's nothing inherently inefficient, wasteful or burdensome about public spending. On the contrary, the public sector is so efficient at doing some things that nearly every country in the world relies on it to do some of the most important jobs. Different nations, at different points in time, have experimented with private fire brigades, judges, police forces and sewerage systems, and it's no accident that most eventually favour public-sector delivery. Of course, not every citizen will agree on the importance of providing some services or the best way of doing so. Take education, for example. While Australian governments spend more money per student than Finnish governments, the Finns are widely regarded as having the best schools in the world. But as there are no private schools in Finland, and in turn no public funding for schools with indoor pools, rifle ranges and dressage arenas, clearly some in Australia consider some of our educational institutions to be far superior to their Finnish counterparts. Quality, efficiency and equity are all a matter of perspective.

The shape of public spending matters more than its size. Just as a teenager who skimps on car maintenance will ultimately learn an expensive lesson, or a stingy manager who allows their best staff to leave will likely harm their business, governments in Australia that underinvest in our people, our infrastructure and our natural environment have been setting us up to fail, not to prosper. But because we heard so much noise about the need to reduce the amount of public spending, we have been denied a genuine democratic discussion about its ideal shape. And the cracks are beginning to show.

The arrival of COVID-19 exposed the fact that some of our schools are so crowded that children aren't allowed to scamper about in the playgrounds or able to wash their hands in the bathrooms. The 2020 summer bushfires showed us that we lack the resources to fight the climate-induced blazes we have fuelled. Rising tensions with China led our Prime Minister to commit to spending 'whatever it takes' to purchase nuclear submarines that will be far more expensive than the $90 billion contract he cancelled with the French. All of this, combined with a growing population that has rising expectations of the available health, education and urban services, means that the amount of government spending, the breadth of assets owned by government, and the scope of government regulation in our lives, are set to expand in the decades ahead. The sooner we admit that, the sooner we can best shape it.

While Australian public debate is full of the droning of non-economists about the 'economic necessity' to tighten our belts and cut government spending if we are to prosper as a nation, when it comes to the size and shape of our public sector, the stakes are much higher than the wobbles of our economic indicators. Long before anyone had ever thought of—let alone measured—gross domestic product, the consumer price index or the unemployment rate, Australia established what would become one of the world's oldest continuous democracies. But the incessant propaganda war against the efficiency and effectiveness of government services, combined with the obsession with shrinking the size and role of governments, is now helping to drive a loss of faith in democracy itself. After decades of vociferous attacks on the idea that government spending and regulation can improve people's lives, is it any wonder that a growing number of people think democracy just doesn't work?

Why would we expect young people, those who've grown up listening to years of derision concerning the role of the state, to have much faith in the ability of their vote, or their collective actions, to solve the big problems they and their country face? Why wouldn't young people turn more to themselves and further away from democracy? Needless to say, the less faith people have in government, and the more people shun the project of democracy, the easier it is for those with power and influence to extract more cash, concessions and corrupt favours for themselves.

~

Who we elect determines which problems we solve. Problems such as reducing greenhouse gas emissions, improving our education system and caring better for our elderly aren't beyond our wit to address, but they have been beyond the want of our elected representatives. In recent decades, the key to winning the most votes in Australia has been to ignore the biggest issues. While this has been frustrating for some, it is important to remember that there is nothing in the Constitution that requires our governments to be far-sighted, competent or fair. Indeed, our Constitution focuses on how to elect members of parliament, not on what they should prioritise once appointed. Yet, despite the lack of any obligation to do so, since Federation, governments of all persuasions have helped our country successfully address significant dilemmas. Government spending, government policy and government-owned assets haven't just improved our lives but saved them as well.

Robert Menzies used regulation and government spending to drive a massive surge in Australian home ownership as well as build the Snowy Mountains hydro scheme, which still delivers power to millions of Australians. Gough Whitlam made university education free and connected millions of suburban homes to a widespread sewerage system. Malcolm Fraser created the Human Rights Commission and the Commonwealth Ombudsman, and he introduced Australia's first *Freedom of Information Act*. Bob Hawke introduced universal public health via the creation of Medicare, and he stopped the damming of Tasmania's Franklin River. All of these leaders wielded the enormous power and resources of our federal parliament to make bold decisions designed to improve the lives of Australians.

But in Australia today, our Prime Minister and his Cabinet spend more time picking small fights than solving large problems. Despite the enormity of the challenges this country faces, from climate change and defence to housing affordability and domestic violence, discussion revolves around slogans, not solutions. And regardless of the overwhelming evidence of history and international experience, the suggestion that government spending, regulation and ownership can significantly improve the lives of most Australians is so derided that it is almost never seriously talked about.

To be crystal clear, I do not believe that governments can or should try to solve all problems. Not only do I want my freedoms, I want more freedoms than I currently have. I want the freedom to die with dignity, and the freedom to criticise my elected representatives without being sued. I want my kids to grow up in a society free from dangerous climate change, particulate pollution, homophobia, racism and sexism. Linking the small size of the public sector to the existence of freedom is like linking the number of plans, roadmaps and strategies a government prints to the existence of a vision for the nation.

Similarly, I also think that governments, like individuals, clubs and companies, can waste money, make terrible decisions, and focus more on the spoils of victory than on the needs of those they are supposed to represent. I don't want to pay taxes and watch them being wasted on offshore detention centres we don't need or on car parks that the private sector could have built. But, like many across Europe, I'd happily pay more in tax and never have to worry about private health insurance ever again.

And just as we shouldn't judge all CEOs according to the behaviour of Gerry Harvey, nor should we believe that just because some politicians are selfish and corrupt, their peers will be similarly self-serving. We must always be sceptical about the motives of our elected representatives, but we must be careful not to become cynical about the role they play. The simple reality is that we cannot have a democracy without politicians. In turn, those who have been led to believe that 'all politicians are the same' have, whether they realise it or not, been led to believe that democracy doesn't work. The project of government is not easy, nor will it always succeed. But democracy thrives on high expectations, and when cynicism about motives replaces scepticism about methods, then only those promising the least will thrive.

Decades of disparagement of the positive role of government in our society has left many conservatives with little more to promise than to keep the levers of power from the hands of those who seek to use them for good. Despite the need to reform our entire energy system, rebuild our straining infrastructure, restructure our unaffordable housing market and redress the deep inequalities that still dominate our society, Scott Morrison's vision for the country is for government to get off people's backs and to prevent Labor from increasing petrol prices, interest rates and taxes. That should fix things.

It is no coincidence that the democratic contest of big ideas has been replaced by debates about costings and modelling and confected culture wars. The determination of so many to eschew the use of the power of the state to solve real problems that affect so many people, means that enormous amounts of political effort and media analysis now revolve around artificial cultural storms taking place in carefully designed media teacups.

Australia, despite our tiny population, comprises the twelfth-largest economy globally. We spend more on defence than all of our nearest neighbours combined. We have enormous amounts of land and natural resources, and the pool of money that has accumulated thanks to compulsory superannuation—a mandated policy you never hear the banking sector complain about—is one of the biggest reservoirs of savings in the world. We can afford to do anything we want, but we can't afford to do everything we want. The big choices are all ours, including the choice of whether we can be bothered to make them.

No-one else in the world cares if we choose to squander our good fortune. Just as the Hawke government's $36 million subsidy for Kodak did nothing to prevent the rise of digital cameras, Australia's $10 billion per year in subsidies payable to the fossil fuel industry will do nothing to stop our export customers from moving away from oil and gas and coal. But while Australia cannot shape the world economy, we can shape where we fit in it. Or not.

In 2013, Australia voted against the rollout of a fibre-to-the-home broadband network and opted instead for one that relied on the existing copper wire network, on the basis that it would be cheaper and nearly as good. And in 2019, Australians voted for a government that promised to spend billions on car parks, sporting clubs and inland rail. Every day, governments make decisions about how much money to spend, and on what to spend it. Decisions to subsidise new drugs can be literally life-saving for some, and the choice not to spend more on acute mental health care will literally cost the lives of others. Likewise, decisions about whether or not to let adults marry who they want, have an abortion if they want, and choose to die with dignity when they want, all have an enormous capacity to shape the lives of millions of Australians. It's hard to believe that anyone who understands how important government decisions are could believe that who is in government doesn't matter.

There never will be a permanent settlement on the optimal size and shape of government. Just as technological and social changes require amendments to laws that are otherwise working well, so too do external events ranging from climate change and COVID-19 to the rise of China in our strategic backyard. Just as those who lead companies, cricket teams or simply their own families must permanently adjust to changing circumstances, opportunities and shifts in preferences, so too must our elected representatives. Good government requires creativity, commitment and constant vigilance.

But Australia's democratic debate has become uncoupled from the real challenges we face. Eight years after being elected to solve an imaginary budget emergency, the Coalition is not only yet to deliver a single budget surplus, it does not expect to do so this decade. Government debt and spending are at record highs and, despite decades of warnings about its dangers, the economy is still growing strongly. Not even the business community, fresh from its enormous serve of JobKeeper, is keen to bemoan the current amount of public spending.

The Coalition wants to spend big on defence. The business community wants the government to spend big on infrastructure and training. And voters want the government to spend more on health, education and tackling climate change. But while there is unanimous agreement that government needs to spend more on some things, there remains a collective denial that the role of government is going to grow significantly in the coming decades. It's time our leaders confronted that obvious truth.

Australia is one of the richest countries in the world, but for decades we have been told we can't afford nice things like free health care, great schools, or public toilets that don't stink. Our population of twenty-five million people is smaller than that of cities like Tokyo, Shanghai and São Paulo, but our economy is bigger than those of countries like Brazil and Spain; in fact, it is only a tiny bit smaller than Russia's. We can afford to have nice things if we want them.

We used to have nice things, via Menzies and his successors, as mentioned earlier. But since John Howard, we've had gruel. For twenty-five years now, Australians have been told that we need to tighten our belts, privatise our services, and stash as much of our own money away in super-annuation as we can, because we can't rely on our government to look after us in the future. Even the fact that, on average, Australians are living longer, healthier lives is seen through the prism of the burden of an ageing population on the Common-wealth Budget rather than the success of our public health system.

Other countries have nice things. Germany offers free higher education not just to all its citizens but to refugees as well. Both France and the United Kingdom provide free universal health care. But although Australia's economy grew rapidly from 1991 until the COVID-19 crisis began in 2020, throughout that whole period we were made to feel poor, like we had to settle for less.

Whether we collectively spend more money buying nice things for each other, or whether our representatives keep cutting taxes for high-income earners, the size of the public sector is set to grow regardless. The big trends putting pressure on our governments are immune to the posturing of pundits and politicians pretending to hold back the tide with a broom. Australia simply cannot keep pace with its allies, its rivals or the challenges it faces if it remains determined to have a smaller public sector than virtually every country it likes to compare itself to.

~

The 1 degree of warming that the burning of fossil fuels has already caused has given Australians a taste of the ferocity and frequency of fires, floods and droughts we can expect as we head for the 2 degree world on which Scott Morrison's 'plan' for climate action is based. And given that the only way to avoid the costs of dealing with those catastrophes is to set a crash course for climate action, if successive governments choose to do little to avoid climate change, they will have no choice but to spend a fortune adapting to it in the century ahead.

The storm that smashed into Collaroy Beach in 2016 washed away more than sand and swimming pools. It swept away much of the apathy about climate change in the wealthy enclave of Sydney's northern beaches. Since that storm, Tony Abbott has lost his neighbouring seat of Warringah, and local Liberal MP Jason Falinski has started to speak out about climate change. Meanwhile, the local council has approved the construction of a 7-metre-tall, 1.3-kilometre-long seawall to protect forty-nine properties at a cost of $25 million. The owners of the multimillion-dollar properties in question have, at a cost of $300 000 each, collectively funded most of the price of that eyesore, with the NSW Government and local governments picking up the rest of the tab. Just as no man is an island, no millionaire can save their property if their neighbours don't chip in. Collective action is the only solution to climate disasters.

The inconvenient truth, however, is that the Commonwealth Government estimates around a quarter of a million homes are at risk of inundation this century. Does anyone think that most of the affected communities, and their local councils, will be able to afford similar protection as the northern beaches residents? And does anyone think that an island the size of Australia can even protect its current coastline from rising sea levels and more powerful storm surges?

Private-sector insurance won't be of much use. The only reason that private companies offer insurance policies is they expect to collect more from worried safe people than they'll spend on those who are actually in danger. As anyone who has ever tried to get hail insurance as a storm approaches knows, once something becomes likely, it also becomes impossible to insure against. And so it is with the costs of climate change. For example, the costs of the damage caused by storms and floods in northern Queensland have been rising rapidly in recent decades and, in turn, so have insurance premiums. Just as young people pay a lot more for their car insurance than older drivers, northern Queenslanders pay a lot more for their home and contents insurance than people in Sydney and Melbourne. At least that's the case when it is the market assessing the risk and setting the price.

In May 2021, Scott Morrison announced a $10 billion fund to help underwrite the risk of offering insurance to households and businesses in northern Australia. When small government rhetoric meets political reality, the fight never takes long. And as Australia's fossil fuel production continues to grow, so too will the costs to Australian governments of subsidising the insurance of a growing population living in increasingly dangerous locations.

Likewise, by the time the 2020 bushfires had finally burned themselves out, they had destroyed 18 million hectares of land and more than 500 buildings, and killed thirty-four people. While Morrison justified his mid-crisis trip to Hawaii on the basis that he didn't hold a hose, when he finally held a press conference he was quick to promise to do 'whatever it takes' to help bushfire victims. But such promises will only become more expensive as our climate heats up. As a downpayment, he committed $2 billion to a new reconstruction fund which, two years later, is yet to reconstruct the lives of hundreds of uninsured people.

As once-in-a-century events begin to occur every decade, or even more regularly, the cost of protecting, repairing and removing buildings, infrastructure and even whole communities will be staggering. The financial cost of the 2020 bush-fires was over $3 billion, and that of the Brisbane floods in 2007 was more than $7 billion. The then federal Labor government introduced a temporary 1 per cent tax levy across the whole country to fund the repairs, but unlike that levy, the costs of climate change aren't going to be temporary. The options facing future governments are to spend more on protecting our lives or a lot more on fixing the damage.

Of course, it is not just the consequences of climate change that will expand the role of the state. Our efforts to avoid climate change, inadequate as they are, are leading to more public spending, government regulation and public ownership of key infrastructure.

John Howard was the first Australian prime minister to introduce a mandate to drive invest-ment in renewable energy, in the form of his Mandatory Renewable Energy Target back in 2004. And while by 2007 he was supporting a mandatory carbon price in the form of an emissions trading scheme, he didn't stay in power long enough to introduce the one he'd promised.

After winning the November 2007 federal election, Labor significantly expanded the MRET, and after weathering the 2010 election it introduced an emissions trading scheme, the $10 billion Clean Energy Finance Corporation and the $1.4 billion Australian Renewable Energy Agency.

The Coalition government has spent a lot of public money on climate issues as well. Tony Abbott defined himself by his preference to rip up Labor's market-based approach to climate policy and replace it with a $4 billion fund to pay polluters to stop polluting. While much of that money has been wasted paying farmers to do what they were going to do anyway, and ultimately it has proved ineffective in reducing emissions, it has been highly successful at expanding the size of government.

And then there's all the nationalisation taking place. The Coalition is set to spend up to $10 billion on the Snowy 2.0 hydroelectric storage system. This is on top of a $1 billion equity injection into the Kurri Kurri gas-fired power station, and the $20 billion inland railway line that Barnaby Joyce has described as 'one of the great carbon abatement policies that goes to show how the Prime Minister and myself and our colleagues are using technology to take this nation ahead'.[1]

Whether it's retrofitting public buildings for electric vehicle charging, protecting whole suburbs from rising sea levels, subsidising the insurance of millions of Australians, or regulating the remediation of tens of thousands of petrol stations around Australia, the response to changes in our climate, including the evolution of our energy systems, will require an enormous increase in the size and scope of the public sector in the decades ahead.

Needless to say, the consequences of climate change are not the only threats we face nor the only major pressure on the size of our public sector. As the smoke from the 2020 bushfires finally abated, the first cases of COVID-19 were making their way to Australia. This new coronavirus, from the same family as the common cold, would go on to kill more than 750 000 Americans, 150 000 people in the United Kingdom, and, thanks to a combination of geography and our willingness to rely heavily on the role of government, 'only' around 2000 Australians. Had Australians died of COVID at the same rate as occurred in the

United Kingdom, around 54 000 of us would have likely perished.

Prior to the arrival of COVID-19, every year Australian hospitals were on the verge of being overwhelmed by the seasonal flu. People needing hip replacements would regularly wait years, emergency wards were often overflowing on weekends, and those needing mental heath or dental care often went without treatment as affordable care was so difficult to access. COVID-19 has increased the pressure on an already stretched healthcare system.

Nobody believes that state and federal governments should invest in less preparations, less spare capacity or less emergency response planning than they did pre-COVID. On the contrary, given that new strains of COVID-19 will keep emerging, along with entirely new pandemics, then if Australia is to avoid the fate of the United Kingdom and the United States, we will need to spend more money on our national health system, not less.

Australia's lack of standalone quarantine facilities led directly to all of our earliest outbreaks, lockdowns and deaths. While private hotels were more effective than home quarantine, they were a poor substitute for purpose-built facilities such as the government-owned and operated Howard Springs, from which no outbreaks were traced. The air conditioning, infection control and even patient transport within our hospital system was not designed with airborne infections in mind. We can either set ourselves the task of improving the air quality in our hospitals, schools, public transport and other public spaces, or we can act surprised when we find ourselves poorly prepared for the next pandemic. Democracy is the way we make such choices.

In the eighteenth century, cities around the world began the radical, monumental task of cleaning up their rivers and drinking water, and building sewerage systems. The only thing that outweighed the enormous cost of these tasks was the enormous benefit of doing so. Today, air pollution and poor air quality is directly linked to around 4 per cent of Australian deaths, is a significant cause of debilitating respiratory illness, and spreads the common cold, seasonal flu and other infectious diseases. Whether or not we choose to act on such knowledge and protect ourselves from the threats with a bigger and better public health system, has everything to do with the kind of society we want to live in and nothing to do with some arbitrary assumption about the ideal size of the state.

~

When two self-driving cars crash into each other, which car owner will pay for the damage? If a company uses artificial intelligence to select new recruits and the algorithm is shown to discriminate against women, who will be prosecuted for breaching anti-discrimination laws? And when people use 3D printers to make exact replicas of patented furniture, jewellery and toys in the privacy of their own homes, how might that be dealt with by the companies which believe their products have been 'stolen', or indeed by the police?

We always need to be drafting new regulations, and we should always be on the lookout for regulations that we no longer need. Regulation isn't good or bad. To suggest that the number of pages of legislation that exist, or the number of new laws that have been drafted, provide some insight into the 'burden' of regulation, is like suggesting that the shorter an instruction manual is, the better it will be.

As new technologies, new problems, even new cultural patterns emerge, governments need to introduce new regulations, modify old ones, and sometimes ditch them altogether. Few mourn the loss of laws requiring car drivers to have someone walk in front of their vehicle waving a red flag, or of laws preventing women from swimming in whatever they feel confident wearing. Some may wish that we still had laws stopping companies from charging different prices to different con-sumers for exactly the same products, but alas, price-discrimination legislation was abandoned in the name of deregulation long ago.

Sensible people agree that some laws are good, some laws are dumb, and some laws need to be updated, but Australian political and policy debate has long been dominated by the meaningless assertion that deregulation is good, red tape is bad, and the best thing that governments can do is get out of people's lives. Leaving aside the hypocrisy of those conservatives who oppose giving individuals the right to die with dignity, have an abortion, or marry whomever they love, there is something deeply flawed in the logic that government regulation reduces economic efficiency and harms GDP growth. It is not only impossible to run an economy without regulation, but those who own and run the biggest businesses are usually the biggest fans of (some) regulation.

Australia needs to have a sensible conversation about which things need more regulation and which things need less. We also need to have a sensible debate about whether we are spending enough money on enforcing the regulations we have. Successive royal commissions and coronial inquiries have found fundamental failings in the way the bodies responsible for overseeing aged care, disability care, foster care, our banking system and the Murray River are resourced and run. While the deeply problematic robodebt system was used to ensure compliance for those on welfare, those who profit from public funding for running aged-care homes are notified well in advance of any inspections, as are providers of disability care and even cosmetic surgeons.

Australians should be able to forward spam emails and text messages straight to a government regulator and expect action to be taken against repeat offenders. We should be able to expect that every hospital, every aged-care home and every foster home is clean and safe regardless of whether it is publicly or privately run. Implementing the recommendations of the royal commissions and other inquiries we have funded will cost tens of billions of dollars per year, but of course it is a democratic choice whether we want to protect the elderly from malnutrition and the disabled from bedsores, not an economic one. If we had no intention of acting on the recommendations of our expensive royal commissions, it's hard to under-stand why we asked for them.

And then there's defence spending. In late 2021, Scott Morrison said he would spend 'whatever it takes' to buy an unknown number of an unknown design of nuclear submarines at an unknown price. In making that commitment, he didn't just give away Australia's bargaining power, he abandoned any pretence of comparing the benefits of a project with its costs.

Australia spends a lot of money on its military. A lot. Taiwan has a population about the same size as Australia's, and it sits less than 200 kilometres off the coast of China, which continues to make a territorial claim over the island state, but we spend about three times as much on defence as Taiwan does. Indeed, Australia spends more on defence than all of our nearest neighbours combined,[2] and, despite their proximity to Russia, more than all the Nordic countries combined as well. Yet despite, or perhaps because of, our enormous expenditure, Australians don't feel very safe, with a recent survey revealing we are almost as worried about a Chinese attack occurring 'soon' as the people of Taiwan are.[3]

The issue goes deeper than an enormous increase in the amount of money spent on traditional defence equipment and personnel. In addition to all the new submarines and fighter jets and tanks that we will likely never use, we are opening up new frontiers, such as the $7 billion announced in 2021 to create the Australian Space Agency, with billions more to be spent on upgrading cyber-security, quantum computing and other measures designed to wage war in new ways. And then there are the laws designed to protect Australians from terrorism, which have led to the removal of a wide range of personal freedoms. In the decade from 11 September 2001, the Commonwealth Parliament enacted fifty-four pieces of anti-terror legislation that restricted the right of individuals to engage in a wide range of previously lawful activities and transactions. The new laws led to the banning of specific organisations and forms of speech. In Australia today, it is an offence punishable by up to five years' imprisonment to refuse to answer questions asked by the Australian Security Intelligence Organisation.

The creation of such laws, primarily by the Howard Coalition government, and usually with the support of the then Labor Opposition, makes a mockery of the oft-stated view that Australian governments have some strong objection to the use of regulation, based on a firm faith in the responsibility of individuals. Both the size and power of Australian governments have grown rapidly in recent decades, but the blunt denial of this simple reality has prevented important decisions about where additional powers might yet be needed and which existing laws have passed their use-by dates.

~

Australia has never had a big public sector. Ever. While it's true that Gough Whitlam boosted spending significantly when Labor took office in 1972, after twenty-two years of Coalition governments, the result was a public sector that was only a little bigger than the moribund one it replaced. It was still quite small by European standards.

There was nothing reckless or unexpected about the one budget deficit Whitlam delivered. He was elected to modernise the country and he rapidly set about introducing free university tuition, building sewers across outer suburbs and providing free legal aid. And while Medicare didn't come cheap, it saved a lot of lives, and a lot of money for ordinary Australians. As a result of his government's new spending measures, Whitlam delivered a budget deficit equivalent to 1.8 per cent of GDP, which is tiny compared to the deficits delivered by Paul Keating in 1991–92 (4.1 per cent of GDP), Joe Hockey in 2015–16 (2.4 per cent) and especially Josh Frydenberg in 2020–21 (7.8 per cent).[4] The size of the Commonwealth public sector was drifting upwards before Whitlam was elected and the trend has continued since.

On the deficit front, not only has Frydenberg never delivered a budget deficit as small as Gough's one and only, the current government's own budget papers suggest he never will. But despite the steady growth in Australia's public sector over the last fifty years, government spending remains low compared with other developed countries, and a lot lower than prosperous countries like Denmark and Sweden.

And yet, despite the clarity of the data, our public and political debates continue to revolve around the imagined need to reign in our low levels of spending and obsess about our relatively small budget deficits. Unless someone has proposed a tax cut—indeed, even after the enormous budget blowout from the COVID crisis, the Coalition government still brought forward tax cuts.

Neoliberalism has reshaped the public sector. It hasn't reduced it. It's often said that if you are going to tell a lie, tell a big one. Well, it's hard to imagine a bigger lie than the assertion that for the last twenty-five years, successive Australian governments have been singularly focused on reducing government spending and the size of the budget deficit. Nothing could be further from the truth.

While there is no doubt successive governments have talked endlessly about the need to protect credit ratings and spare future generations the 'burden' of public debt, in reality their desire to cut taxes, subsidise the industries they like, substitute expensive consultants for relatively cheap public servants, and take pride in pork-barrelling, has seen both Commonwealth spending and deficits increase as a percentage of national income—that was the case even before the COVID crisis hit. Put simply, as a percentage of GDP, the Abbott/ Turnbull/Morrison governments never once spent less than the Whitlam government, but a half-century after Gough, the party that paid $40 billion in JobKeeper allowances to companies whose revenues were growing still argues that

Labor comprises big spenders who can't be trusted with other people's money.

According to the International Monetary Fund, treasurer Peter Costello was the most profligate spender in modern Australian history.[5] Having slashed spending on health, education and welfare in the late 1990s on the basis of needing to pay down debt, when the mining boom of the early 2000s filled the Budget with new revenue, Howard and Costello chose not to restore the expenditure they had slashed but instead introduced enormous cuts to income tax, company tax and capital gains tax. They also outlaid a lot of money on subsidising private schools, private health insurance and, of course, defence. They didn't cut the public sector—they cut spending on their enemies and gave money to their friends.

The 1990s are often referred to as the 'golden era' of policy reform, but the so-called achievements of that era don't hold a candle to the steady growth and low unemployment underpinned by the Keynesian spending policies of Menzies, or the radical reform era of Whitlam, much less the corporatist reforms to the industrial relations system of the early

Hawke years, or the Labor–Greens minority government that delivered a carbon price, the National Disability Insurance Scheme, world-leading cigarette packaging changes, and a royal commission into sexual abuse within the Church. Apart from cutting taxes, privatising a lot of assets, and subsidising the private provision of services that were previously managed by the government, the lasting legacy of the 1990s is a broad suite of economic policies and institutions that continue to fail in their stated aims.

The *Competition Act* has failed dismally to create competition in Australia, resulting instead in highly concentrated, and highly profitable, banking, retail, transport and electricity industries that charge high prices by world standards. The much-vaunted intergenerational reports created by Peter Costello as part of his 'charter of Budget Honesty' embraced a narrow focus on the (highly exaggerated) costs of ageing while virtually ignoring climate change, the ultimate test of intergenerational equity. And, most miserably, the so-called Productivity Commission has overseen a collapse in Australia's productivity growth to the lowest levels on record. As treasurer, Scott Morrison promised not just a big boost in productivity but annual accountability to ensure he was on track to meet his big pledge—needless to say, he made good on neither.[6]

There's no doubt the reform agenda of the 1990s has many powerful fans, especially among the Treasury economists who dreamt it up, and the self-appointed business leaders who benefited personally from the lower taxes, lower wage growth and reduced competition it delivered. In fact, to this day, the designers and beneficiaries of the National Competition Policy hark back to those 'unfinished reforms' when the abject state of Australia's recent economic performance is raised. But it's clear from the available evidence that we need to break with the past, not revisit it.

~

Leaving aside the fact that the Chinese Communist Party has obviously delivered much higher rates of economic growth than Australia's Coalition government, even among democracies it is clear that the countries with the biggest public sectors are doing a better job of managing their economies and their societies than those with the smallest. The big-spending Nordic countries—which include Finland, Norway, Sweden, Denmark and Iceland—don't just have higher living standards, longer lives and happier populations than Australia. They have experienced higher productivity growth as well. It's as if, without slashing spending on health and education, or privatising key infrastructure, they have somehow found a way to deliver health and wealth to their populations. Who'd have thought?

In 1990, the average Australian worker produced slightly more GDP per hour worked than the average worker in the Nordic countries. GDP per hour worked is the most common measure of labour productivity, and boosting this productivity has been at the heart of Australian industrial relations, tax and education policies for decades. But despite, or more likely because of, our obsession with cutting taxes for high-income earners, slashing public spending and reducing the role of unions in our workplace, the rate of productivity growth in the Nordic countries has been much higher than that in Australia. High wages, high taxes and a big public sector don't burden the Nordic economies, they propel them. The Nordic countries aren't just richer and happier than Australia, they're also more innovative, with strong manufacturing industries.

Volvo recently presented the world's first vehicle produced entirely from coal-free (or zero-carbon) steel from Swedish steelmaker SSAB. While the Australian Government argues that producing more coal, more gas and more 'plans' for net zero will 'lead' some form of transition to a low-carbon economy, other countries are actually investing more money in the technologies that will drive that transition (as opposed to delaying it). At the same time, they are creating both incentives and obligations to prompt companies and consumers to change their spending patterns. It's not complicated, it really is Economics 101, but it's not happening here in Australia.

Economists generally believe that good education is the key to driving productivity growth in the long run, and so it comes as no surprise to learn that the Nordic countries, with some of the highest rates of productivity in the world, are also renowned for having the best education systems. But what few Australians likely realise is that there are almost no private schools in those countries, their teachers earn significantly higher wages than they do in Australia, and their universities are completely free. Oh, and they have free or virtually free child care as well. Somehow, the fact that the countries with the best education systems in the world rely almost exclusively on the public sector to educate their children, from preschool to post-doctorate, has had precisely no impact on the design of Australian education—none. The evidence is so bright that successive education ministers dare not gaze at it. Either Australians really love our privatised child care, expensive (yet subsidised) private schools, and how our kids leave university with debts the size of some overseas home loans, or our elected representatives are really letting us down.

For just $42 500 per year, a shade over the minimum wage, you can send your child to Geelong Grammar, if they like the look of you.

Despite its sprawling 245-hectare waterfront campus, the school has an indoor Olympic-size pool, just in case. Indoor tennis and hockey courts help ensure that kids can work their wriggles out even when the weather isn't as nice as the landscaping. The equestrian centre has a large indoor arena as well, which caters for students who are interested in dressage, eventing and show-jumping—it's good to offer kids choices. Both the federal and Victorian governments give public money to Geelong Grammar, as well as to Australia's other private schools. Significantly, all of the money spent on everything from grounds-keepers to dressage instructors is included in the national accounts under 'education'. And we pretend to be confused about why our system lags behind that of the Nordics.

Of course, not all schools are so lucky. Science students at Canberra's Lyneham High can't use Bunsen burners because the school's gas pipes need replacing, although compared to some schools' inability to provide soap in their bathrooms, perhaps this limitation on science experiments is nothing to grumble about. And while Nordic schools have pioneered outdoor and active education for primary school students, some Australian schools are so crowded that kids aren't allowed to run in the playground. Not at Geelong grammar, mind you. Just at overcrowded public schools.

The reason that Australian schools don't perform anything like the Nordic schools is that, after thirty years of neoliberal 'reforms', the two systems look nothing alike. While successive state and federal governments have raged about the need to lift productivity over those same decades, the fact that we were spending billions to increase the amenities at our elite schools and pretending we couldn't afford to boost the wages of public school teachers, or provide air conditioning or build nice playgrounds, was somehow overlooked. Australians have come to believe that government spending on elite private schools is fair because if the private school kids went to public schools instead, it would cost the government money. By that logic, we should presumably give money to car owners who promise not to use public transport, and to people who don't use wheelchairs and who promise not to use ramps.

Nor is there any evidence that indoor pools and equestrian centres improve education outcomes in the short term or productivity in the long term. But, luckily for those who benefit from such policies, no-one has ever suggested they should. When it comes to being fair to the rich, we don't ever have to worry about whether we can afford it or whether it works. Only the poor need to prove their worth.

The upshot is that, where other countries provide free child care, great public schools and free post-school education, Australia relies on expensive subsidies to private providers of schooling, and of vocational and tertiary education, all of which are still free to charge expensive fees. That's why our educational performance is slipping, traditional apprenticeships are declining, and female participation rates lag those of major European countries. And still, despite the obvious failures of decades of an increasing reliance on a subsidised private sector to take the place of the public sector, the most common prescription for Australia's economic malaise is to venture further down the neoliberal path. As the then secretary of Treasury, Martin Parkinson, told us back in 2014:

> The productivity challenge requires a wide ranging and comprehensive response, of which tax reform is a key part. Taxes, of course, detract from how efficiently the economy operates ... But it's also important that this public debate, as with all good public debate, is grounded in the facts.[7]

If only it was. The facts don't show that taxes 'detract from how efficiently the economy operates', and Martin Parkinson knows that. Taxes on tobacco, alcohol and fuel capture negative externalities and increase efficiency. Taxes on windfall gains don't distort decision-making at all, and Treasury itself has proposed carbon taxes, mining taxes and a range of others. Dr Parkinson might have personal preferences regarding which taxes he likes most and which ones he likes least, but his overt hostility to the important role of tax is proof of how captive we have become to ideology dressed up as economics.

~

Tax is an investment in society. It is the way in which individuals contribute to collective national projects. It not only delivers high returns in its own right, it literally makes returns from other investments possible. Expenditures on public health, education, sanitation and infrastructure don't just make it possible for individuals to live and work but are literally essential for the establishment and growth of new economic activity. If low taxes were the main driver of investment, then the economies of Iraq, Myanmar and Yemen would be booming, and high-tax countries like Sweden, Denmark and France would be economic backwaters.

Virtually everything Australians have been told about their tax system is nonsense. Our income tax rates are low compared with those of other developed countries, including Denmark, France and Austria, which have a top personal income tax rate of 55 per cent and have no trouble attracting and retaining highly skilled workers. Indeed, more people migrate from low-tax Iraq and Yemen to high-tax Europe than the other way around.

The Morrison government, like the Rudd government before it, has set a cap on the amount of tax it wants to collect. Like a dieter who can't resist the biscuit tin, it seems our leaders can't trust themselves to only collect as much as they need. But just as diets don't work for most people, our arbitrary tax–GDP ratios don't work for our governments, our economy, or our society either. Decades of tax cuts have delivered low productivity growth, low wage growth, declining school rankings, long hospital waiting lists and, not surprisingly, the budget deficits that those who love the tax cuts profess to hate.

There is no right amount of tax that a country should collect—even if a government believes this is the case, there is nothing in any economics textbook that will help it select such an amount. The current 'cap' of 23.9 per cent came about in 2017. If we had randomly selected 24.9 per cent, then the Commonwealth Government would have had an extra $20 billion per year to spend. And if the Commonwealth collected a similar proportion of the tax collected in the Nordic countries, then it would have around $100 billion extra to spend each year on any of the problems it deemed worth solving, including tackling climate change, buying even more defence equipment, or even reducing debt if it wanted to.

It is true that, while individuals, companies and state governments need to accumulate money from income or borrowing before they can spend it, that is not the case with governments that can literally print their own currency. However, while that simple observation is a source of great passion for some, its significance is easy to overstate.

The Australian Government can literally never go bankrupt, as it can always print currency to repay its debts, but it is not true that governments can simply fund as much public-sector spending as they want by printing more money. The total amount of stuff that can be produced by a country each year is limited by the size of its workforce and the available skills, machinery and infrastructure. No matter how much money it prints, a country like Australia can always make more stuff each year than a country like Kiribati and less than a country like China or the United States, but the more tax a country collects, then the bigger its public sector will be able to be.

As the amount of stuff a country produces each year is limited by the extent of its workforce, infrastructure and other real resources, if the Commonwealth Government tried to double the size of our health, education and aged-care sectors without restricting the amount of money spent by the private sector (via an increase in tax collections), then the result would simply be a surge in inflation—as the government and private sectors bid with each other for the same workers—rather than a surge in the quality of services.

In simple terms, neither taxes nor printing money actually 'fund' Commonwealth Government spending, but while increasing taxes makes room, so to speak, for more public spending, printing more money does not. When there is high unemployment and lots of other idle resources in the economy, then an increase in public spending without an increase in tax can mop up the spare capacity without driving inflation. But when unemployment is low or inflation is already rising, then more taxes are needed to offset more public spending.

Taxes are the main way in which governments reshape their economies. The countries that collect the most tax have the biggest public sectors, and in turn, they have the highest-quality health and education systems. Countries that heavily tax tobacco and alcohol have lower rates of smoking and drinking, and countries that tax wealth and income at the highest rates have the least inequality between those with the most and those with the least. While there is no evidence that collecting more tax harms economic growth, there is overwhelming evidence that collecting more tax redistributes income and can have a transformative effect on society. That is precisely why tax system design is a democratic issue, and it's also why so many powerful people in Australia have spent so much time ensuring that this is presented as an economic issue.

If Australia scrapped the $10 billion per year it spends on subsidising fossil fuels and instead invested the same amount of money in publicly owned renewable energy and storage, we would rapidly reduce greenhouse gas emissions and at the same time drive down energy prices and build assets that would deliver dividends for decades to come. If Australia reigned in the $9 billion per year it currently spends on capital gains tax discounts and instead spent the same amount building housing for those fleeing domestic violence and those working in aged care in very expensive suburbs, among other people, we would dramatically reduce housing costs and the prevalence of inequality, and again, build valuable long-term assets. Taxes and government spending don't ruin the economy, they reshape it, so you can see why those whose wealth is tied up in fossil-fuel extraction or a rental-property portfolio fear the so-called burden of a bigger government.

Taxes always have, and always will, play an essential role in economics, from defining the size of the public sector to shaping private-sector production and income distribution. Tax policy lies at the heart of the democratic project, which is precisely why so many people in power want to pretend it's an economic issue that is for them alone to address.

~

The war against public services has been fought on many fronts in Australia. We have been bombarded with pseudo-economic claims that both public spending and the associated tax revenue are inherently inefficient, and the moral attacks have been just as vicious. Australians have been trained to believe that there is something shameful about receiving most government services, except the ones it's OK to be proud of.

Robert Menzies never shared that view. In 1944, the founder of the once liberal Liberal Party told parliament:

> The moment we establish, or perpetuate, the principle that the citizen, in order to get something he needs or wants and to which he has looked forward, must prove his poverty, we convert him into a suppliant to the state for benevolence … That position is inconsistent with the proper dignity of the citizen in a democratic country. People should be able to obtain these benefits as a matter of right, with no more loss of their own standards of self-respect than would be involved in collecting from an insurance

company the proceeds of an endowment policy on which they have been paying premiums for years.

Oh how we have moved on from there. Some recipients of government support and services are demeaned in Australia, with the unemployed being called 'job snobs', and Indigenous people being forced to use the Indue card to buy only 'basic items' with the money to which they are legally entitled. Others, meanwhile, have prestige heaped upon them. While the allocation of status is harder to pin down than the allocation of public spending, it's still pretty easy to spot whose public support comes with a side serve of shame and who simply gets to enjoy the perks of office.

Take public housing, for example. Taxpayers provide Scott Morrison with not one but two houses for him and his family to use. Most university vice-chancellors in Australia are given nice digs as well. And the Commonwealth Government has a whole agency dedicated to providing for a group of public servants deemed worthy not just of public housing but high-status lodgings: the

Australian Defence Force. Doubtless, the need for defence personnel to move around the country for work is a good reason to provide them with public housing, but the fact that we choose to do so with no reported stigma, or alleged financial burden on the state, is proof that the shortage and shame associated with the rest of Australia's public housing is a choice, not a necessity. We simply do not support teachers, nurses, women fleeing domestic violence or new migrants as well as we support defence personnel. Such choices are literally what democracy is all about.

We haven't always made such choices—many countries around the world still don't, and likely never will. Past Australian governments, state and federal, Labor and Liberal, have relied on the full suite of housing policies common in other countries, including rent control, large-scale public housing construction, and government-backed rent-to-buy initiatives. Building houses when the economy slows down is a great way for governments to stimulate the economy at a time when others are choosing not to build. It's not complicated. But the voices of government in Australia are the only ones that focus on housing as a cost rather than as an investment. The main skill of a property developer is to anticipate government zoning decisions, secure finance, and oversee a bunch of subcontractors. Not only do state and local governments have better access to information, finance and contract oversight capacity than any property developer, if they want to they can provide a guaranteed source of tenants as well. As the annual accounts of the 100 per cent Commonwealth-owned Defence Housing Authority clearly show, it's not hard for government-owned property developers to build and buy the houses they want, in the locations they want, and to make them available to the people they want—with no stigma.

There is no constitutional or financial obstacle that prevents the DHA from building even more homes and making them widely available, nor is there ambiguity about the role of the DHA, which describes its objective as being to 'provide adequate and suitable housing for, and housing-related services to, members of the Australian Defence Force ... and their families'. Wouldn't that be nice for other Australians.

Governments around the world, including those here in Australia, know how to develop housing, lease it and sell it at a profit when they want to. But for decades, Australians have been told that it is not the role of government to do so. Who says? Such an opinion is not based on economics and it has never been put to a referendum. On the contrary, opinion polls suggest the public is supportive of such an 'expansion in the role of the state', or to put it another way, citizens are supportive of governments making a profit out of developing properties for people who need them. Yet, rather than invest heavily in publicly owned housing that can be provided to whichever groups we think need it most, Australian governments are more likely to sell off their public housing stock. Indeed, the NSW Government was so determined to sell off some prime public housing that it couldn't even be bothered renovating it first—talk about putting ideology ahead of income.

The Sirius building was an architecturally acclaimed public housing high-rise in Sydney's The Rocks district which offered some tenants panoramic views of the harbour. But rather than renovate the building for its existing residents, or oversee the redevelopment of the real estate to capture significant capital gains for taxpayers—which is what any other owner with deep pockets and no rush to sell would do—the NSW Government simply evicted the public housing tenants, including a 92-year-old blind woman, and let a private developer take all of the profits from the refurbishment. Less than two years after the last tenant was removed, the developer was taking out glossy full-page advertisements in *The Australian Financial Review* boasting about how the newly spruced up apartment complex had been 'reimagined for a modern sensibility, with a level of luxury its harbourfront address deserves'. Australian governments clearly don't think war widows, the disabled, or those who have lost their jobs, deserve nice things like a view, or housing that's close to public transport and the CBD.

But imagine if, during another phase of the COVID crisis, or the next downturn in the construction industry, our state and federal governments stimulated the economy via the creation of beautiful public housing rather than through tax cuts for high-income earners or JobKeeper payments to firms whose profits are going up. Imagine if every time the economy turned bad, we invested in things that made people's lives good. Just as our gorgeous, Depression-era, Art-Deco ocean baths still delight local residents nearly a century after they were built, there is absolutely no reason why our suburbs, including the 'nice' ones, can't benefit from new construction designed to simultaneously house and beautify our communities.

The disparity between how we house soldiers and how we house pensioners highlights the strategic way in which not just money but shame is allocated by Australian governments. There is no indignity for soldiers in living in 'public housing'; there is no embarrassment when they contact the Department of Veterans' Affairs to access their welfare benefits and public health services. There is no economic or administrative reason why Centrelink could not administer the payments and services meted out by the DVA. It's just that the primary purpose of the department isn't administrative or economic in nature, it is cultural, sparing our vets the humiliation of queuing for hours with those whom we have decided to humble.

In the words of the Productivity Commission, 'Australia supports veterans with a separate and beneficial system.' In explaining the unique occupational nature of military service, the PC identifies how members of the armed services:

- are required to follow orders—members are subject to military law and discipline and are not as free as other Australians to make independent decisions or to choose to avoid personal injury in armed conflict
- have authority to apply lethal force against enemy forces
- are frequently placed in high-risk environments, including in war or operational service and while in training or on peacetime service.

Those who suffer physical and mental trauma while defending Australia against threats deserve our perpetual appreciation and support, but a large number of other Australians are owed similar levels of care. People who have suffered physical, sexual or mental violence, both in domestic and other settings, were certainly not free to make independent decisions at the time, and often remain in high-risk environments for many years. We could help them if we wanted to—likewise, people who have worked in our hospitals, jails, ambulance services and police forces, and those who have volunteered to fight fires or work with vulnerable groups, all of whom face a high risk of experiencing post-traumatic stress disorder. The belief that Australia is a poor country that must choose which groups of people we can afford to help forces us to think in terms of categories of the 'most deserving'. However, once we acknowledge that Australia is a rich, low-tax country that can afford to spend billions in public money on car parks and sporting clubs, it is easy to understand that, if we wanted to, we could design a health system that gives all Australians the care they need, not just the 'most deserving'.

On a sinking ship with a shortage of life jackets, it would make sense to ask the question 'Who needs them most?' Similarly, in a crowded hospital emergency ward, it makes sense to consider whether we should treat the heart-attack victim first, even if the guy with the sprained ankle has been waiting for hours. But Australia is not in a crisis. We are rich beyond our imaginings. We just spent $200 billion on COVID measures and were told (rightly so) that this wasn't a big deal for a country of our size. Crisis thinking keeps us divided, distracted and deceived. It's no accident we are encouraged to use it.

Neoliberalism has trained Australians to focus on how deserving individuals are, rather than on how caring we think our society should be. We take it for granted that pensioners get more income support than the disabled, who in turn get more than the sick, who in turn get more than the unemployed. We know that the unemployed don't get cheaper groceries or petrol, but we also think that if we are too generous towards them, they won't look for work. So we decide that we have to be cruel to be kind—except when it comes to the provision of subsidies to Geelong Grammar.

Shame lies at the heart of the design and differentiation of our public services. That's why we don't make veterans use the Centrelink office, much less retired politicians who need to inquire about their generous pensions for life. While the budget papers spell out who gets the money and who does not, it's far less clear who gets chastened and who gets the blind eye turned their way. Few Australians would disagree that single mums, the unemployed and people with mental health conditions are made to feel like a much bigger drain on the budget than retired politicians, judges or veterans.

~

Shame has been used to deter us from seeing direct government service provision as the solution to many of our problems, and pride and fear have been used to steer Australians away from demanding better regulation. As the Prime Minister who introduced a $66 000 fine for Australians returning from India during the COVID crisis said, 'Australians are sick of being told what to do by governments.'

Australians have been taught to scoff at the idea that regulation might improve our lives, our communities, our environment and our economy. Endless calls for deregulation, promises to cut red tape, and platitudes about individuals being freed from the burden of regulation, have crowded out room for a sensible conversation about what things we want to regulate more or less, and better ways to implement the regulations we already have. Yet economics students are taught that regulation is essential if markets are to even exist. Put simply, without the strong regulation of property rights that define who owns what, and how that ownership can be protected and transferred, no capitalist would spend a cent building a new factory or creating new medication. Companies would cease investing.

Of course, our governments and business leaders know that. They just frame regulations that powerful people want as good and regulations that powerless people want as bad. No-one uses the words 'red tape' to describe laws that give the Catholic Church the right to discriminate against gay people. Indeed, the Coalition has been enthusiastic in its use of such laws to limit the freedom of unions, environmental groups and charities to participate in public debates. As they say in Russia, 'For my friends, anything. For my enemies, the law.'

Big companies don't hate regulation, they love it. Apple sued Samsung for making a smartphone that was rectangular in shape, I kid you not. Qantas relies on regulation to 'own' a particular shade of red. Philip Morris tried to use international trade regulations to sue Australian governments over the introduction of plain-packaging regulations that made it harder for the tobacco giant to promote its deadly products. Mining companies love regulations—they sue each other, and protesters, all the time. The profits of the big banks are protected by a mountain of regulation preventing competitors from opening up. In fact, the big banks are currently arguing for much stronger consumer protection laws to apply to financial technology firm Afterpay, not because they are trying to stifle competition, of course, but because these noble institutions—which the Hayne Royal Commission determined were selling dodgy products to disabled people and charging fees to dead people—just want to ensure that Afterpay isn't ripping off customers.

Organisations that can afford lots of lawyers love lots of laws.

Not all regulation is good. While I for one am a fan of regulations that prevent Australians from buying machine guns and selling methamphetamine, I have no problem with deregulating the sale of marijuana (one of the world's most-traded commodities in the eighteenth century), voluntary euthanasia, or the ability of supermarkets to employ pharmacists and dispense medicines. As a rule, I'm pro-choice and pro-competition, but in Australia, because I'm opposed to churches imposing their dogma on citizens and to big companies exploiting their market power, I'm called a radical lefty. I don't mind what I'm called, but it does bother me that name-calling is such a winning strategy in Australian public debate.

I understand why some people are concerned that marijuana might be a gateway drug. I understand why some people want to protect the right of pharmacists to make us wait for long periods of time while standing in their overpriced retail environments before handing us the pills our doctors prescribed. Obviously I don't share those concerns, but I'd happily debate them. Unfortunately, slogans about small government have been used to silence sensible opinions about which kinds of regulation really are necessary and which ones aren't. The only thing worse than dogma is dogma inconsistently applied.

Most people think that Google and Facebook have accumulated too much power, make too much profit and pay too little tax. Back in the late nineteenth century, US consumers, along with politicians, thought the same thing about JD Rockefeller's Standard Oil, which by 1890 controlled 88 per cent of all oil refining in America. After the introduction of strong competition regulation, Standard Oil was compulsorily broken up into a number of much smaller companies, which today include Chevron, Mobil and Amoco. At the time of the break-up, JD Rockefeller was the richest person in the world.

Breaking up monopolies doesn't ruin economies, it builds them. Indeed, the entire obsession with privatisation back in the 1990s was allegedly based on the premise that breaking up government monopolies would deliver lower prices, higher quality and more choice to consumers. Needless to say, most privatisations delivered higher prices, lower quality and less choice, but that was the fault of the Productivity Commission and Treasury officials who were more focused on maximising the sale price of the assets they were selling than on actually delivering the benefits of competition. In 1974, Gough Whitlam introduced Australia's first restrictions on cartels and other anti-competitive conduct that had been tolerated since Federation. Big business was far less excited about that criminalisation of price fixing, bid rigging and a wide range of other profitable practices than they would be, years later, about the 1000 pages of new industrial relations legislation that John Howard introduced in the name of 'deregulating' the labour market. Like beauty, the necessity of all regulation is in the eye of the beholder.

But it is not just the moribund ideological assertion that the regulation of big business harms our freedom and sense of pride that holds Australia back. We also have been trained to be afraid of big companies, or more opaquely, of the markets punishing us for daring to put our preferences ahead of their profits. To be clear, it's the monopolies that exploit their market power and buy up all their competitors that are inefficient, not the laws required to stop them. Firms that make huge profits in Australia and pay little or no tax aren't helping our economy either, they are helping their shareholders. We know how to address these issues, but we've been scared off or shamed away from doing so.

In 2019, the federal Coalition government introduced what it called 'big stick' regulations for the energy market. These gave the treasurer the power to request the Federal Court to force privately owned companies to sell off key assets if the treasurer thought they were abusing their market power. This forced divestment is exactly the kind of power the US Government used to break up Standard Oil back in the 1890s. And in 2021, the Coalition legislated the News Media Bargaining Code, which forced Google and Facebook to negotiate payments for content with Australian news outlets ranging from News Corp to *The Guardian*. Under the code, if the tech giants couldn't come to an agreement with the news outlets, then compulsory binding price arbitration would be used to set a fair price. Google threatened to quit Australia, and Facebook shut down its newsfeed for a day, but now that the code is in place, the tech giants have spent an estimated $100 million paying for content they used to get for free. Meanwhile, the Australian media, while still under pressure, is recruiting staff in numbers that haven't been seen for years. So it's simply not true that little countries like Australia can't take on big companies, but such myth-making has aided powerful corporations and simultaneously harmed Australian consumers for a long time. Bizarrely, we have ministers who are more eager to stand up to the Chinese military than they are to confront foreign gas companies over the lack of tax they pay.

Contrary to much of what is written about them, the biggest companies in the world aren't bigger or more powerful than countries like Australia, not even close. Claims that their revenues dwarf the GDP of countless nations are, like the descriptions of most of the crap they sell, deliberately misleading. It's just silly, like a gorilla beating its chest, or the Australian mining industry exaggerating the size of its workforce. In 2020, Alphabet (the owner of Google) made a profit of $51.9 billion and Facebook made a profit of $37.6 billion. Australia's GDP that year was $1929 billion. In short, the income of Australia is thirty-seven times bigger than that of Google and fifty-one times that of Facebook. Plus, we have an army, spy services, a continent, and the ability to print our own currency. If Google is 'powerful', what adjective should we use to describe Australia?

Why, then, do we fear the wrath of companies with far less income, far less resources and far shorter time horizons than our own? Australia spent four years fighting in World War I, six years fighting in World War II, and twenty years in Afghanistan and Iraq. Facebook's boycott of Australian news sites—and the advertising revenue attached to them—lasted a day.

Capitalist economies, and civilised societies, are built on the regulation of individuals, companies and governments themselves. The design of that regulation needs to be in a permanent state of flux as priorities, preferences and technologies change. Asking whether Australia needs more or less regulation is like asking if twelve is a big number: it seems precise but it's actually meaningless.

Parts of our society, environment and economy need more regulation and parts need less, and resolving which is which is a democratic issue. The decisions to ban asbestos mining and whaling were quite harmful to those who worked in mining and whaling. Alternatively, the decision to force people to allocate 10 per cent of their income to superannuation has created a huge number of jobs in the finance industry. Some regulations cost jobs and some create jobs. As with tax, which activities we want to regulate more heavily and which ones we want to deregulate are democratic choices the Australian people should be consulted on, not economic rules Australians should be lectured on.

~

It wasn't just the Commonwealth's Keynesian stimulus that got Australia through the COVID-19 crisis. Without the services of the 100 per cent government-owned Australia Post and the 100 per cent government-owned National Broadband

Network, hundreds of thousands of businesses, big and small, not to mention our school system, never would have been able to pivot to online delivery. Just imagine if Australia Post had already been privatised. Would the owners have doubled their parcel-delivery capacity, or would they simply have doubled their prices and profits?

Government in general does a good job of running a wide range of businesses. Just as calls to cut government spending are often code for redirecting where government money is spent, the same is true of privatisation. We have privatised lots of services that low-income earners rely on. However, Australia is in the midst of a nationalisation boom. It's just not considered polite to talk about it.

When he was treasurer, Peter Costello was keen to sell off the Commonwealth Government's last shares in the Commonwealth Bank, but his ideology didn't prevent him from establishing the $170 billon funds-management business called the Future Fund, which he now chairs. Similarly, while Tony Abbott was hostile to Labor's fibre-to-the-home model for the NBN, he wasn't opposed to creating a government-run company to build and own it, a company valued today at more than $30 billion. The current Coalition government has been on its own nationalisation spree over the past eight years. Its investment in the Snowy 2.0 scheme, which is owned by the entirely government-controlled Snowy Hydro, is projected to total around $10 billion, which will more than double the size of the current publicly owned company. Also consider the 100 per cent government-owned Australian Rail Track Corporation, which has assets of around $4.5 billion and ultimately will itself own the $30 billion worth of inland railway that has been championed by Barnaby Joyce.

As with government spending and regulation, Australians have long been told that governments just aren't any good at running businesses, except of course when powerful people want to run them. Time will tell whether Tony Abbott's NBN and Barnaby Joyce's inland rail are white elephants or white-hot investments, but there is no doubt that our government has the ability to build nationally significant businesses from scratch and run them efficiently. The fact that it also has the capacity to waste enormous amounts of money is not an indictment of the ability of the public sector but of the judgement of our elected officials.

True, it's not just governments that can run things badly. The United Kingdom is currently undertaking the re-nationalisation of some of the railways it privatised back in the 1990s. Still, here in Australia, some of the companies we privatised on the basis that this would drive down prices seem to have made huge profits instead. Whoops.

Imagine if the Commonwealth Government was as willing to spend billions of dollars developing renewable energy, battery storage, electric-car-charging facilities and, literally, rewiring our suburbs as it is to invest billions in new diesel railway lines through National Party seats?

Imagine if Australia Post could provide you with a permanent email address and default super-annuation, banking, insurance, electricity and phone plans which were free to use or could just be ignored. Imagine how easy and cheap it would be to switch and compare services, and imagine how much the big brands that make billions from your confusion and apathy would hate it.

Imagine if you could forward all the spam you get on your phone and in your inbox straight to a government regulator who had the resources and resolve to track down who was sending it and do something about it.

Imagine if all of our public schools and public hospitals were so good that you wouldn't feel pressured to spend tens of thousands of dollars per year on private schools or private health insurance.

Imagine if all ABC content was provided for free over our NBN, as was all of the research from our publicly funded universities. What better way to improve the quality of debate than to make publicly produced information freely available to all Australians.

Imagine if governments spent big on building things like housing and renewable-energy batteries whenever the economy slowed, so that we created jobs during downturns and infrastructure that would deliver benefits for generations to come.

Contrary to popular belief, there is nothing in economics textbooks that says the private-sector provision of goods and services is necessarily more efficient than public-sector delivery. Nothing at all.

Indeed, introductory textbooks dedicate whole chapters to helping students understand the very predictable situations in which market failure can occur and, in turn, the circumstances in which government regulation or provision is superior to market outcomes. However, thanks to the stultifying policy architecture handed down from that 'golden era' of the 1990s, Australian policy-makers systematically turn a blind eye to the existence of market failure in Australia and pretend that public spending, regulation and ownership is inherently inefficient when the real problem is its increasingly poor oversight and administration by ministers who are overtly hostile to the positive role of government.

Reform is not inevitable. Those on top of a rigged game never think it's time to change the rules. Those who've never seen the game played well are prone to tuning out rather than learning more. And those who fear the consequences of their past behaviour will fight harder to prevent accountability than most people will fight to ensure it.

Who we elect determines what problems we fix. Just as there is no right amount of government spending, nor a right amount of regulation, there is no right answer to which issues our elected representatives should seek to resolve and which they should ignore. Unfortunately, Australians have allowed their democratic deliberations, such as they are, to remain focused on technocratic issues of how best to solve a narrow range of problems, rather than on the democratic issue of which problems we should fix.

Assertions that the public sector is too big and that money is too tight have been used for too long to constrain the scope of democratic debate in Australia on these matters. Many Australians now believe that it doesn't matter who they elect, in part because they believe all politicians are the same. But even if politicians all had the same degree of intelligence, empathy and commitment, it is inconceivable that they would all bring the same priorities and concerns with them on their way into parliament. Scott Morrison's priorities mattered when he chose to focus on legislation to enshrine the right of churches to discriminate over legislation to create a federal anti-corruption watchdog. Likewise, his priorities mattered when he went with his preference for nuclear submarines over his contract and relationship with France. Politics matter, who we elect matters, and what direction they drive our government in matters.

It is impossible to predict the likely future shape of the Australian public sector, but it is inevitable that it will grow in absolute terms, and it is almost inevitable it will grow as a proportion of GDP in the decades ahead. This is not a problem to be feared but simply a reaction to the fact that, as people get richer, they want more of the services like health, education and aged care that governments are better at providing. Just as the share of agriculture declines in the economy as people get rich enough to spend far more on restaurant meals than they ever spent on vegetables, the size of the state will grow for as long as people think that their kids deserve better education and their parents deserve better aged care than what is currently dished out.

The size of government will continue to grow at least as fast as our rapidly swelling population. However, it is not at all inevitable that the governance and oversight of government will grow at all. When John Howard took office in 1996, annual Commonwealth spending was around $139 billion and today it is more than $588 billion. After decades of 'downsizing', our local, state and federal governments between them now employ more than 2.1 million people. But while the public sector has grown, our governance, the number of sitting days for federal parliament, the government of the day's responsiveness to issues raised in Question Time and in writing, freedom of information requests, even demands by the parliament for the release of documents—all have declined markedly. It's now time to hit pause on reforming the economy and focus instead on reforming our parliament and our democracy.

Surely those who want to see less government spending in general and those who want to see more money spent on their priorities can both agree that Australia needs much better scrutiny and oversight of the way in which public money is spent. And surely both groups can agree that only those who benefit from poor oversight and governance would resist calls for their improvement. Similarly, those who would see Australia spend far more on defence and border protection, and those who would see a more humane approach to refugees and a much bigger social safety net, should be able to agree that collecting more tax revenue from foreign oil companies and other international entities is a clear win for Australia, regardless of how the spoils are distributed. As shown by the tripartisan support for the News Media Bargaining Code that forced Google and Facebook to invest in Australian journalism, when Australians work together, they have no difficulty in taking on so-called global giants.

Our democratic institutions, just like the economy, need continuous care, maintenance and, from time to time, reform. Yet, unlike the economy, we barely even talk about the health of our democratic institutions, culture or outcomes, except to note their steady weakening.

As I stated earlier in this book, democracy thrives on high expectations. We are bound to be disappointed by the actions of individual politicians and governments, but disappointment and cynicism don't change anything. Unless large numbers of citizens are willing to change their votes in response to practices and attitudes they disagree with, then there is no reason for them to expect their elected representatives to change their behaviour. The suggestion that all politicians are the same is really suggesting that democracy doesn't work, which is clearly not the case. Changes in governments have made big changes to Australia.

Of course, it is harder to make good decisions if we don't have good information. To that end, the auditor-general is appointed by the governor-general, on the advice of the prime minister, for a ten-year term. Uniquely, the auditor-general reports directly to parliament via the speaker of the House of Representatives and the president of the Senate, with the Joint Committee of Public Accounts and Audit approving any recommendation for appointment. But the government of the day has complete control over the budget for the Australian National Audit Office, which supports the inquiries of the auditor-general. Between 2013 and 2021, the budget for the ANAO was cut by more than 20 per cent in real terms, leading current Auditor-General Grant Hehir to state that some government agencies might only be scrutineers once every two decades.

Just as there is no right size for the public sector, there is no right size for the ANAO, but an annual budget of less than $80 million with which to scrutinise expenditure of more than $500 billion per year does seem a trifle small, especially when you consider that just one of the Commonwealth's VIP jets costs $74 million—and we have three of them. The government also spends more than $100 million per year on advertising and more than $800 million on detaining asylum seekers offshore. If we really wanted to spend more on auditing the effectiveness of government spending, we could afford to do it.

A phoney fight has raged for decades about the need to shrink the size of the Australian public sector, which has been growing all the while. But as the shape of our public services has changed radically, for many Australians its efficiency has declined markedly. For many, queueing for hours to speak to Centrelink, waiting years for elective surgery, senior citizens suffering from malnutrition in publicly funded aged-care homes, have become the norm. And while these issues are all blamed on a lack of funding, what is really missing is oversight, accountability, and ministers who actually take responsibility for what happens on their watch.

Democracy is the place where ambitious politicians and apathetic voters come together to shape and sustain their local community, their state, their nation—for the politicians, it can also be about their place in history, their infamy or, most likely, irrelevance. From the vantage point of modern Australia, with its anti-vaxxers on the streets, its inability to create a federal corruption watchdog or implement meaningful climate policy, and with our Prime Minister being called a liar on the world stage, it's hard to believe that in decades past our country managed to fight world wars, create a universal healthcare system, grant native title, and, far more recently, legalise same-sex marriage, without tearing the country apart—albeit, we did make it through the COVID-19 pandemic with one of the lowest death rates in the world.

Democracy works when we use it well. We must beware the siren song of cynicism and technocratic explanations for failures of will and resolve. New Zealand has both Twitter and a far less acrimonious political culture than ours. The United Kingdom has the Murdoch media and yet climate policy is uncontroversial. The Nordic countries aren't perfect, but their very existence rebuts the absurd assertion that collecting lots of tax and spending lots of money on your population is bad for the economy.

The role of the state needs to evolve according to changes in priorities, preferences and technology, and so too must our democratic structures evolve over time to suit the needs of our population and the practices of our politicians. The rules of cricket were revised in response to the English innovation of bodyline bowling, or aiming directly at the batsman, and the rules of Rugby League likewise were changed to prevent head-high tackles. It is up to our democracy to develop new rules and sanctions to protect itself from the threat of those who would seek to use the levers of government primarily to cause misery for their foes rather than to create prosperity for all.

Our elected representatives must be reminded of their legal obligations, and voters must be reassured that their public services, no matter their size or shape, are being well managed. This can be achieved at least in part through such things as the creation of a federal corruption watchdog, one with teeth; a bigger, better auditor-general; parliamentary committees with the ability to compel consultants as well as public servants to answer questions and provide documents; and the restoration of a commitment by public servants to store and disclose rather than shred and conceal documents—to name just a few initiatives. People would also care more about governance if they cared more about the point of government. After all, government policy potentially saved tens of thousands of Australians from dying from COVID, just as Australian Government–funded research led to a vaccine for cervical cancer.

The size of government is not an end in itself. It should vary, over time and between countries, depending on the circumstances a nation finds itself in, the priorities of its citizens, and the impact of new technologies on the relative ability of the government, companies and individuals to solve different problems. But nevertheless, the size and shape of government are among the most important choices a country can make, and it is time the Australian public was consulted about them. If our democracy and our economy are to thrive, we will need to find a way to draw the public back into these decisions.

The government will get bigger in the coming decade. The important question is whether it will get better. Ultimately, that's up to us.

ACKNOWLEDGEMENTS

Thank you to Ben Oquist at The Australia Institute for giving me both the time to write this essay and the title it needed. Luckily for me, Ben often has a knack for seeing more clearly what I'm trying to do than I do. My sincere thanks also to Louise Adler for believing not just in the essay but that it could be delivered as quickly as we promised. And special thanks to Paul Smitz for his firm editing and his gentle project management.

Essays like this are a long time in the making, if not in the writing, and while so many conversations have shaped it, my colleague Dave Richardson was responsible for many of them, as was Ben and my endlessly patient parents, who have long disagreed with most of my conclusions but have always supported my determination to express them. What more could a son want?

And then there's my boys. In addition to tolerating my incessant typing and providing endlessly welcome distractions, my two sons Henry and Wilkie have both helped me realise just how important our public schools are. Wilkie's research into Nordic schools was particularly important, and I hope one day more kids get the space and time to climb and play, which Wilkie craves and the data supports.

And finally, thanks to all the supporters of The Australia Institute who make all my work possible, and all the people on Twitter and Facebook who help keep me informed, inspired and on my toes. Social media isn't a sewer, it's a powerful new voice that we are all learning to deal with. Just like the role of government, the role of the media will always keep changing, which is as it should be.

For much of the research that sits behind this essay, more information about The Australia Institute, or to donate to fund its research, visit its website (https://www.australiainstitute.org.au).

NOTES

1   Phillip Coorey, 'Barnaby Says Inland Rail Good for the Planet, Keeps Net Zero Alive', *Financial Review*, 31 August 2021, https://www.afr.com/politics/federal/barnaby-joyce-says-inland-rail-will-be-good-for-reducing-emissions-20210831-p58nky (viewed December 2021).

2   According to the Stockholm International Peace Research Institute, Australia spent more on defence than Indonesia, Thailand, Malaysia, the Philippines, New Zealand, Fiji and Papua New Guinea in 2020.

3   Daniel Hurst, 'Australians Fear Attack from China almost as Much as Taiwanese Do, Survey Shows', *The Guardian*, 9 July 2021, https://www.theguardian.com/world/2021/jul/09/australians-fear-attack-from-china-almost-as-much-as-taiwanese-do-survey-finds (viewed December 2021).

4   Australian Government, *Budget 2021–22*, budget paper no. 1, statement 11, pp. 353–77, https://budget.gov.au/2021-22/content/bp1/download/bp1_bs11.pdf (viewed December 2021).

5   Paolo Mauro, Rafael Romeu, Ariel Binder and Asad Zaman, 'A Modern History of Fiscal Prudence and Profligacy', IMF working paper 13/5, January 2013, https://www.imf.org/external/pubs/ft/wp/2013/wp1305.pdf (viewed December 2021).

6   Scott Morrison, 'Protecting Our Living Standards', address to CEDA, Canberra, 24 October 2017, https://ministers.treasury.gov.au/ministers/scott-morrison-2015/speeches/address-ceda-canberra (viewed December 2021).

7   Martin Parkinson, 'Enhancing Our Living Standards through Tax Reform', speech to Business Council of Australia/PwC Tax Reform Forum, Sydney, 11 September 2014, https://treasury.gov.au/speech/enhancing-our-living-standards-through-tax-reform (viewed December 2021).

IN THE NATIONAL INTEREST

Other books on the issues that matter: